Keep this little book
with you as an antidote
to stress wherever you go.

Find inspiration in its
quotations and feel your mind
relaxing as you color its images.

Calm will return.

Talent develops in quiet places.

JOHANN WOLFGANG VON GOETHE

A thing of beauty is a joy for ever.

JOHN KEATS

A journey of a thousand miles
begins with a single step.

Nurture your mind with great thoughts.

Benjamin Disraeli

Forgetting oneself is opening oneself.

DŌGEN

Learn to let go. That is the key to happiness.

ANONYMOUS

Fall seven times. Stand up eight.

You cannot perceive beauty but with a serene mind.

HENRY DAVID THOREAU

Nature does not hurry, yet
everything is accomplished.

Lao Tzu

In a mind clear as still water,
even the waves, breaking, are
reflecting its light.

DŌGEN

I always prefer to believe the best of everybody; it saves so much trouble.

RUDYARD KIPLING

To climb steep hills requires a slow pace at first.

WILLIAM SHAKESPEARE

To enjoy—to love a thing for its own sake and for no other reason.

LEONARDO DA VINCI

Minds are like parachutes. They only function when open.

LORD DEWAR

He is a wise man who does not grieve for the things which he has not, but rejoices for those which he has.

EPICTETUS

I believe a leaf of grass is no less than the journey-work of the stars.

WALT WHITMAN

The power of imagination makes us infinite.

JOHN MUIR

Nothing we see or hear is perfect. But right there in the imperfection is perfect reality.

SHUNRYŪ SUZUKI

He who lives in harmony with himself lives in harmony with the universe.

MARCUS AURELIUS

To the mind that is still, the whole universe surrenders.

Lao Tzu

Meditation and water are
wedded for ever.

HERMAN MELVILLE

Genius is eternal patience.

MICHELANGELO

Be yourself; everyone else is already taken.

OSCAR WILDE

Simplicity is the glory of expression.

WALT WHITMAN

Life is beautiful, as long as it consumes you.

D. H. LAWRENCE

Nothing is so strong as gentleness, nothing so gentle as real strength.

SAINT FRANCIS DE SALES

Only through art can we emerge from ourselves and know what another person sees.

MARCEL PROUST

Quiet thoughts mend the body.

CHINESE PROVERB

Wherever you go, go with all your heart.

CONFUCIUS

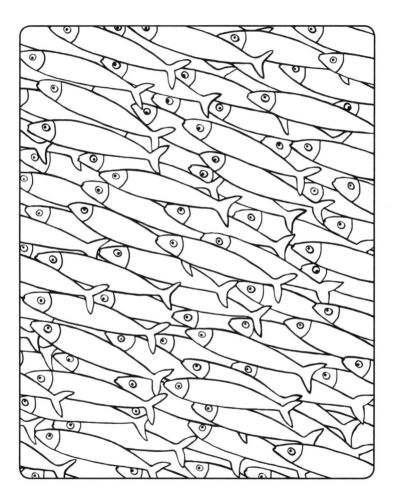

Hitch your wagon to a star.

RALPH WALDO EMERSON

Cease worrying about things which are beyond the power of our will.

EPICTETUS

You can never cross the ocean until you have the courage to lose sight of the shore.

CHRISTOPHER COLUMBUS

Our life is frittered away by detail . . . Simplify, simplify.

HENRY DAVID THOREAU

Inspiration and imagination go hand in hand.

ANONYMOUS

Never give up, for that is just the place and time that the tide will turn.

HARRIET BEECHER STOWE

If a thing loves, it is infinite.

WILLIAM BLAKE

You are the universe in ecstatic motion.

RUMI

Sitting quietly, doing nothing,
Spring comes, and the grass
grows by itself.

ZENRIN KUSHÛ

The energy of the mind is the essence of life.

ARISTOTLE

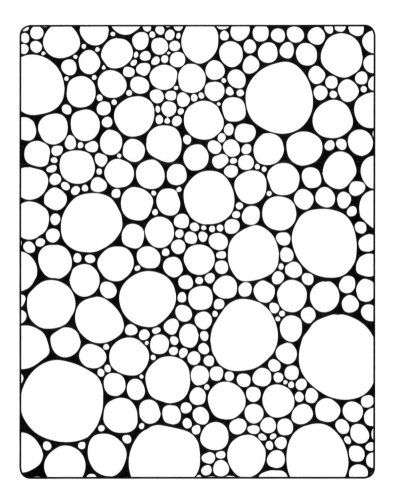

Wonder is the beginning of
wisdom.

SOCRATES

All appearances are illusions.

BODHIDHARMA

This world is but a canvas to our imagination.

Henry David Thoreau

Nature does nothing without purpose or uselessly.

ARISTOTLE

After a storm comes a calm.

PROVERB

Keep your eyes on the stars, and
your feet on the ground.

THEODORE ROOSEVELT

Fast is fine, but accuracy is everything.

Xenophon

You will never make a crab walk straight.

ARISTOPHANES

Take rest; a field that has rested gives a bountiful crop.

OVID

The reward of a thing well done
is to have done it.

RALPH WALDO EMERSON

It does not matter how slowly you go as long as you do not stop.

CONFUCIUS

Man must be disciplined, for he is by nature raw and wild.

IMMANUEL KANT

Variety's the very spice of life,
that gives it all its flavor.

WILLIAM COWPER

Do not feel lonely, the entire universe is inside you.

RUMI

However long the night, the
dawn will break.

AFRICAN PROVERB

In wildness is the preservation of the world.

Henry David Thoreau

May I be safe.

May I be healthy.

May I be happy.

May I live with ease.

BUDDHA

The ocean is a mighty harmonist.

WILLIAM WORDSWORTH

Time flies never to be recalled.

<small>V</small>IRGIL

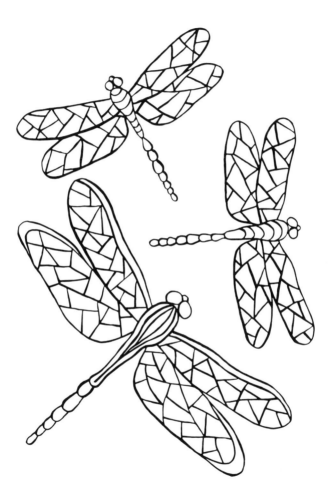

There is nothing either good or bad, but thinking makes it so.

WILLIAM SHAKESPEARE

Every great achievement was once considered impossible.

ANONYMOUS

I dwell in Possibility.

EMILY DICKINSON

The trees that are slow to grow
bear the best fruit.

MOLIÈRE